HAPPY
AND
GLORIOUS

Hilary McKay grew up in Boston, Lincolnshire, the eldest of four girls in a family devoted to books. After reading botany and zoology at St Andrews University she switched to English. In 1992 she was joint winner of the Guardian Children's Award for THE EXILES, her first novel picked from the publisher's "slush" pile! THE EXILES is the prequel to THE EXILES AT HOME which won the Smarties Award in 1994. Hilary now writes full-time and lives with her maths teacher husband and son and daughter, Jim and Isabella, in Derbyshire.

Also by Hilary McKay

HAPPY
AND
GLORIOUS

Hilary McKay

Illustrated by Hilda Offen

a division of Hodder Headline plc

Text Copyright © 1996 Hilary McKay
Illustrations Copyright © 1996 Hilda Offen

First published in Great Britain in 1997
by Hodder Children's Books

10 9 8 7 6 5 4 3 2 1

A Catalogue record for this book is available from the British Library

ISBN 0340 64074 X

Typeset by
Phoenix Typesetting, Ilkley, West Yorkshire

Printed and bound in Great Britain by
Mackays of Chatham plc, Chatham, Kent.

Hodder Children's Books
A Division of Hodder Headline plc
338 Euston Road
London NW1 3BH

CONTENTS

To Caroline with love from Hilary

UNOFFICIAL BIRTHDAY

One morning the Queen woke up very early. It was her Unofficial birthday. (Queens have two birthdays, one on the day they were born on and one on the day that it would have been more convenient for them to have been born on. It is the convenient one that counts.) The Queen (who was inconveniently ten that day) thought they should both count but no one else in the palace agreed.

"Happy Birthday to you," she sang as she sat up in bed and tried not to remember this sad fact.
"Happy Birthday to you,
Happy Birthday dear good gracious Your Majesty!
Happy Birthday to ME!"

And though it was only half past five in the morning she jumped out of bed and rushed off to wake her Ladies-in-Waiting.
"It's my birthday!" she called through the keyholes of their doors.

7

The Ladies-in-Waiting pushed their fingers in their ears and took no notice.

"It's my birthday!" shouted the Queen, bouncing on their bed. "Presents!" she added encouragingly and tugged at their blankets.

"It's only your Majesty's Unofficial Birthday!" snapped the Ladies-in-Waiting and they stuffed their heads under their pillows and went back to sleep.

The Prime Minister and his wife lived in a rent free flat over the palace kitchens. The Queen rang the bell and whacked on the door with the edge of her crown until the Prime Minister crawled out of bed and opened it.

"Happy My Birthday," said the Queen putting her crown back on. "I've come for my you-know-what."

"What?"

"What I wrote on the list that I gave you yesterday."

"What list ducky?" asked the Prime Minister's wife. "You ought to have your slippers on!"

"That list of what I want most for my birthday of course," explained the Queen crossly.

"Oh THAT list!" said the Prime Minister. "Well, strictly speaking one could hardly call it a list since only one item was written on it! However . . ."

"And it was shockingly written as well," put in his wife. "Fancy a great big girl like you who can't spell . . ."

"However, however, however," continued the Prime Minister impatiently, "you don't get presents on your Unofficial Birthday so that dispenses with the problem altogether."

It was not a happy morning at the palace.

"We have this trouble every year," groaned the Prime Minister's wife.

"It gets worse," agreed the Ladies-in-Waiting, "because she gets up earlier and so the day is longer."

"It's not as if she 'adn't been told," said the cook.

"And I only asked for one thing!" grizzled the Queen for the hundredth time. "One small present! One cheap present! One easy to wrap up present!"

"*Not* very easy to wrap up!" remarked the Prime Minister's wife.

"We can't get you presents on your Unofficial

Birthday," explained the Prime Minister over and over again. "It would set a Royal Precedent!"

"So what?" asked the Queen.

"So we would have to do it every year!"

"That would be quite all right," said the Queen.

"It would be quite all wrong. You have your presents on your Official Birthday."

"Never what I ask for though," grumbled the Queen. "Rotten boring presents are all I get!"

"Well!" exclaimed the Prime Minister's wife and the Prime Minister and all the Ladies-in-Waiting. "That's not a very nice thing to say!" And they gave the Queen an early lunch and sent her to bed until teatime.

"And then let's see a smiley face!" said the Prime Minister's wife as she closed the Royal Bedroom Door.

There was a balcony outside the Queen's bedroom window with a beautiful view over the Palace gardens. As soon as the Prime Minister's wife had closed the bedroom door the Queen hopped out of bed and went onto the balcony. She leaned over the edge and cried. Nobody took any notice. The Ladies-in-Waiting had all gone to bed with headaches and the Prime Minister was day dreaming about all the jobs he would rather have than being Prime Minister.

"If only I had been more clever at school!" he sighed.

The Prime Minister's wife was making a very small Unofficial Birthday cake. It had no icing and no candles.

Underneath the balcony Michael the gardener's boy was weeding a bed of radishes.

"One of the beastly population!" thought the Queen, and moved over a bit so that her tears splashed on to his head.

"Rain!" thought Michael a moment later, and pulled his cap over his ears.

"OH BOO HOO!" sobbed the Queen.

"Thunder too,' thought Michael without looking up.

"OH HOW SAD I AM!" bellowed the Queen as loudly as she could, and at last Michael noticed her.

"Fine day Your Majesty!" said Michael taking off his cap and bowing courteously over the radishes. "I hope you're having a Very Happy Unofficial Birthday," he added, and he politely did not look at all the tears that were dripping around him.

"I'm having an awful one!" wailed the Queen. "No surprises! No cake! No presents from the Ladies-in-Waiting! No presents from the Prime Minister! No presents," she said staring rather hard at Michael, "from the population!"

"Well, I never," said Michael.

"No and nobody never," sobbed the Queen. "Should be a law against it!"

"There is," said the Queen. "I made it myself."

"Well then," said Michael.

"But they've all broken it," said the Queen. "The pigs!"

"Well never you mind," said Michael, pulling down his cap and wiping his radishy hands on the back of his trousers. "I'll get you a birthday present from the population before tonight or my name's not Jack Robinson!"

And straight away he set off running as fast as he could down the garden path.

"But I thought your name was Michael!" shouted the Queen after him.

"Michael Jack Robinson!" the gardener's boy called over his shoulder.

"I haven't told you what it is I want!" yelled the

Queen, but it was too late. Michael Jack Robinson had already vanished round the corner.

Through city streets and country lanes trudged Michael, collecting donations for the Queen's Unofficial Birthday Present. Some people asked to see his identification and others pointed out that he should have a proper tin instead of a carrier bag, and quite a few said that they were communists or about to leave the country, but on the whole he did quite well. By the time he reached the end of the last lane of the last village his carrier bag was nearly full and he had come to the sea. Far out on the empty beach stood a donkey and beside it, holding up a sign that read

DONKEY RIDES

was the last member of the population.

"Well," thought Michael to himself. "I suppose I ought to finish off the job properly," and he started across the sands.

The donkey's owner had a strange and ruffianly look about him.

"Twenty p a ride," he called to Michael. "Fifty p to make him stop, seventy p to make him gallop, one pound fifty to . . ."

"I'm collecting money for the Queen's Unofficial Birthday Present," said Michael.

"Keep him for life," the donkey's owner had been about to say when he caught sight of Michael's bulging carrier bag.

"How much money have you got there sonny?" he asked.

Michael, although more resourceful than many and more intelligent than most, had not yet acquired the wisdom that prevents one from revealing to ruffianly strangers the exact amount of cash in one's possession.

"One thousand eight hundred and ninety two pounds eighty four," said Michael.

"Fancy that!" said the ruffianly looking stranger, getting onto Michael's money side. "Just twopence short of what you'd need to buy Her Majesty a nice little donkey!"

"I wasn't . . ." began Michael, but it was too late. The ruffianly looking stranger had pushed the donkey into Michael's arms and grabbed the carrier bag.

"I'll put in the twopence!" he called, and disappeared over the horizon.

It was a very long way back to the palace.

Sometimes the donkey carried Michael.

Sometimes (more often) Michael carried the donkey, for he dare not risk wearing out the Queen's one and only very expensive (already rather worn out) Unofficial Birthday Present.

At five minutes to midnight and not for the first time the Queen climbed out of bed.

"What a rotten birthday!" she grumbled, stamping her feet across the bare marble floor.

"What a rotten population!" she sighed, blowing her nose and wiping her eyes on the heavy velvet curtains.

"Michael Jack Robinson," she wrote on the mist on the windowpanes, "is a PIG." And leaning over the windowsill she peered once more down into the empty courtyard.

Surely that was somebody coming down the garden path?

"Michael?" the Queen asked herself and hurried out onto the balcony.

"It *is* Michael!" she exclaimed joyfully.

"And he's got something! Something alive!" she whispered to herself as Michael came closer. "It's got

15

legs! It's wriggling!" and her heart began to thump with excitement.

"Michael you've got one!" she shouted and ran back through the palace and down the stairs to the front door yelling, "He's got one! He's got one! Don't bother to wrap it up!"

"Got one what?" asked the Prime Minister who had fallen asleep in the hall.

"One Donkey!" called the Queen. "Like I put on my list!" And she rushed out into the garden.

16

All the long way home Michael had been trying to think of the best way of explaining to the Queen that he had spent one thousand eight hundred and ninety two pounds eighty-four pence on a second-hand donkey. Glancing nervously up at the palace windows where all the Ladies-in-Waiting and the Prime Minister and his wife were glaring down into the courtyard he began the speech he had prepared.

"I'm sorry . . ."

"He's *just* what I wanted," said the Queen, and she hugged and hugged her donkey.

"Is he?" asked Michael astonished.

"Only better," said the Queen. "Softer. Beautifuller."

"*Is* he?"

"Perfecter!" said the Queen.

"Good," said Michael. "That's a relief."

THE ROYAL DONKEY

The Queen had a donkey that she loved with all her heart. A small grey donkey that had arrived on her birthday when all hope of a birthday present had left her. A silver nosed donkey with fur as soft as thistle down and eyes as dark as a night in the woods. But he was very thin.

Before he came to the palace he had had a very hard life, staggering under loads of sticky children all day, up and down a sandy beach. Since he became the Queen's Royal Donkey everything had changed completely. The Queen would have nothing but the best for her birthday present and on the very first morning of his life in the palace she had kicked the straw out of his stable and demanded carpets instead.

"Straw!" she exclaimed scornfully to the Royal Groom as she staggered backwards and forwards from her bedroom with her arms full of pillows and satins sheets. "Nobody sleeps on straw nowadays! I bet even *you* don't sleep on straw do you?"

"Well, no I don't, your Majesty," admitted the Royal

Groom. "I has sheets and blankets and such, although not such satiny ones as these!"

"Well, *you're* not the Royal Donkey," replied the Queen crushingly.

The little stable grew magnificent. It had green carpets and golden curtains and pictures of the seaside on its walls.

"The pictures are for in case he gets homesick," explained the Queen.

The donkey's bed was satin and eiderdown, very soft and comfy. When the donkey saw it he lay down on it straight away.

"I shall take care of him all myself," announced the Queen. "I shall get his dinners and brush him and tidy his stable and do everything because he is mine and I'm NOT sharing!"

"He's going to take a bit of feeding up," commented the Royal Groom, prodding the Queen's birthday present with a stubby finger.

"Well I *shall* feed him,' said the Queen crossly. "Stop poking!"

"And what his training's been I couldn't say," continued the Royal Groom. "A firm hand will be what he needs I don't doubt . . ."

The Queen glared at the Royal Groom but he took no notice.

"And a good hard going over with a stiff brush every day and plenty of . . ."

"You mind your own business," interrupted the Queen who never enjoyed being given advice, "or I'll . . ."

She did not say what she would do but she looked at the Royal Groom's head as if she didn't care much whether it remained where it was or not.

Since this was not at all how the Royal Groom felt about his head he hurried away to mind his own business in another part of the stables, and the Queen sat down beside her little donkey and brushed his fur with her best hairbrush until his coat glimmered like moth wings.

At first the Queen was very happy, sitting on the pillows beside her donkey and stroking his soft coat but after a time she couldn't help noticing that everyday the donkey grew thinner and thinner and lay on his pillows for longer and longer and looked more and more sadly at the Queen when she came in with his tray. He drank very little and ate nothing at all.

"Just try one little bite!" the Queen would say, and she would eat a bit herself to encourage him, but the donkey just groaned and turned his head away. As the days passed the Queen began to look very worried and she lost all her bumptious ways. The Royal Groom saw her wandering round the stables and thought she looked quite forlorn. Nevertheless he still minded his own business and kept out of the way. Only Michael the gardener's boy came to see the donkey. He had heard that he was ill and had made him a notice. It read,

Pray silence for the Royal Donkey

"I thought perhaps he needed quiet," explained Michael.

"Look at your lovely notice," whispered the Queen to the donkey, but he did not look.

Finally the donkey stopped standing up at all. He nearly stopped moving. He nearly stopped opening his eyes. Even the Queen, who knew very little about donkeys, knew what would happen next if nothing was done. Sobbing and wailing she ran for the doctor.

"I don't usually do donkeys," he told the Queen but he came anyway.

The Prime Minister, sensing a national crisis, followed after the doctor, and the Prime Minister's wife came in case it was domestic trouble and the Ladies-in-Waiting tagged along too and so did the Royal Groom and Michael. Only the Cook, who was far too busy cooking (and anyway hated outdoors), did not follow after the doctor.

"Food disappears as fast as I can cook it these days," she grumbled. "I've no time to waste staring at donkeys!"

Everyone else had plenty of time to waste. They crowded round the stable door while the doctor felt the donkey's heart and looked at his tongue and the Queen cried dismally and the donkey did nothing at all. Underneath his fur he was quite pale.

"He's very thin," remarked the doctor. "But he has no cough, no spots, no fever and no sore throat. And you say he eats nothing at all?"

"Nothing at all," said the Queen, wiping her tears from the donkey's face.

"And drinks nothing at all?"

"Nothing but a small glass of water the day before yesterday."

The Prime Minister sighed and closed his eyes (which proved it was a National Crisis) and his wife mopped her nose and all the Ladies-in-Waiting sniffed and gulped. Two sad tears squeezed out from the donkey's closed eyes.

"I fear there is nothing we can do," pronounced the doctor. "It is obviously All In The Mind."

Everyone groaned and instinctively clutched their heads but the Royal Groom gathered his courage and asked, "Do you think he might be homesick your Majesty?"

"He can't be," sighed the Queen. "He wouldn't even look at his pictures of the sea. I had to put up Rural Churches instead."

"And he won't eat anything at all?"

"Nothing at all," replied the Queen sadly. "See for yourself!"

And she opened the door of the little room where she kept the special donkey equipment to show the Royal Groom all the things the donkey would not eat.

The shelves of the little room were piled high with plates of uneaten food.

There were untouched jellies and bacon and eggs.

Steak pies and fish and chips and soup and bananas. Cold roast chicken and fresh cream trifles. Cups of tea and coffee and chocolate. Bags of nuts and bottles of sauce. Sardines on toast and cauliflower cheese. Cold salmon souffles and curries and puddings. No wonder the cook had found herself so busy.

"I've tried everything!" said the Queen.

The donkey smelt the smell that came out of the little room, a smell like a banquet on a rubbish heap, and he gave a great sigh of hunger and despair. The crowd at the door, overcome by the fragrance of the donkey's left over dinners all fainted in a heap on the ground outside, except for Michael and the Royal Groom. Michael ran for a wheelbarrow to carry away the plates and the Royal Groom jumped to his feet and fetched a bucket.

"Is he going to be sick?" asked the Queen.

The Royal Groom hurried off again and came back with a sack and a battered tin and a box of eggs. The donkey opened one eye and looked at the sack.

"What are you doing?" asked the Queen as the groom poured oats into the bucket and added treacle out of the tin and bran and raw eggs and hot water.

"Wait and see," said the groom.

"Yucky pucky!" said the Queen as he stirred it all up with a wooden spoon. "Go away! You'll upset the donkey!"

But the donkey opened both eyes and sniffed.

"Is that your dinner?" the Queen asked the groom. "I wouldn't eat that for a thousand crowns!"

But the donkey sat up and licked his chops and stuck his head in the bucket.

"Aah!" said the Royal Groom. "Look at that!"

"Oh!" said the Queen and then she stared and stared and then smiled and smiled and all the while dreadful slurping champing noises came out of the bucket.

"They like their grub plain, do donkeys," said the Royal Groom, and there was a long silence, broken only by the sound of chewing.

"I didn't know," said the Queen humbly, and she kicked the doorpost in an embarrassed sort of way.

"I know a lot about donkeys," she said eventually and she looked deep into the oat sack so that the Royal Groom could not see her face.

"You know more than most," agreed the groom tactfully.

"Brushing them," said the Queen, coming out of the sack a bit, "and stroking them and plumping up their pillows, I've done all that. Haven't I?"

"You've done it lovely," said the Royal Groom kindly.

"I've got a good cook," continued the Queen, "at least, she says she's a good cook and she should know. But she never cooks donkey food. What *is* donkey food?"

"Oats and hay and raw carrots and grass mostly does them very nice," the Royal Groom told her.

"No, we never have those at the palace," admitted the Queen, coming out of the sack and sitting down worriedly beside her birthday present. "I wonder what they drink!"

"Donkeys?" asked the groom. "Water."

"Water?" asked the Queen astonished. "Hot or cold?"

"Cold," replied the groom.

"Fizzy?"

"Plain," said the groom firmly. "Out of a bucket."

"Ice?"

"No ice."

"Lemon?"

"No lemon," said the groom.

"Goodness!" said the Queen, and she looked very respectfully at the little grey donkey.

"Tough as old boots, is a donkey," the groom told her.

"Are they?'

"Tougher," said the Royal Groom. "Tougher! Tough as old . . . as old . . . as Old Ladies-in-Waiting!"

"No!" exclaimed the Queen. "They can't be!"

"But with kinder 'earts!" said the groom.

KIND QUEEN

In the palace kitchen someone was singing loudly.

> "Lavender's blue diddle diddle
> Carrots are green.
> I am the Queen diddle diddle
> I am the Queen!"

"Carrots aren't green," said the Cook.

"They're partly green," replied the Queen. "It depends which end you look at and anyway nothing rhymes with orange."

"They're more orange than green," said the Cook who was in a particularly complaining mood that morning.

"Oh alright!" said the Queen cheerfully and she sang,

> "Lavender's blue diddle diddle
> Carrots are more orange than green
> I am the Queen diddle diddle
> I am the Queen!"

"I think I shall go mad!" said the Cook when the Queen had sung it through eight or nine times.

"When?" asked the Queen interestedly.

"One of these days," replied the Cook gloomily. "Look at the state of that dress you're wearing! And there's bits of carrot all over the floor. Give them to me to do!"

"No!" said the Queen chopping and chopping and sucking her fingers. "These are for my donkey. You would never do them properly!"

"Anyone," said the Cook, icily nasty, "can chop carrots into messy modges!"

"I'm cutting them into daisies. You would never bother!"

"Daisies for a donkey!" sniffed the Cook.

"The Royal Donkey!" corrected the Queen. "My Birthday Present!"

"Very nice for some," grumbled the Cook, "to have a birthday!"

"Don't Cooks have birthdays?" asked the Queen surprised. "I thought even Cooks would have birthdays!"

"So they do," agreed the Cook, "and they spend them slaving away in dismal kitchens for people who think the most important thing in the world is the Royal Something Donkey!"

"The Royal What Donkey?"

"Just the Royal Donkey," said the Cook, subsiding into tears. "A very nice birthday I'm having I must say!"

"Good," said the Queen absent-mindedly.

"Or I should say," continued the Cook as the tears ran down her chin and splashed onto her front, "a very nice birthday I'm NOT having!"

"Is it your birthday today?" asked the Queen. "I'd have bought you a present if I'd known." She stopped chopping for a moment to look at her Cook. "Some hankies perhaps, or a comb!"

"You are very unkind!" said the Cook.

"Me!" exclaimed the Queen. "I'm very KIND! Look at all these daisies I've made for the donkey!"

"Well, you're only kind to the donkey!"

"I'm KIND to everyone," said the Queen grandly. "Even Cooks! Kind Queen, that's what they call me! I'd give you anything you like for your birthday but you look like you *need* hankies and a comb!"

"Would you give me anything?" asked the Cook, blowing her nose on a tablecloth and tidying her hair with a fork. "Anything?"

"I expect so," said the Queen vainly. "I am *so* kind!"

"Would you give me the day off?"

"Oh," said the Queen, rather put out. "I'm afraid that would be impossible."

"There!" said the Cook. "I knew!"

"You *are* the Cook," explained the Queen. "That's Fate! You are it, like I am the Queen. So how could I give you the day off? I haven't got a spare Cook."

"Must there always be a Cook?" asked the Cook unhappily.

"If there wasn't," said the Queen working it out on her fingers, "there would be a Queen and someone having a day off and a gap where a Cook should be. I'm afraid gaps are impossible!"

"*You* could fill the gap!" suggested the Cook recklessly.

"Then there should be a gap where the Queen should be!"

"*I* could fill that gap," said the Cook wildly. "We could swop! For my birthday!"

"Lucky for you," remarked the Queen, "that I am a Kind Queen. An Unkind Queen would cut off your head for cheek!"

"But you are a Kind Queen!" the Cook reminded her cunningly.

"Yes I am," agreed the Queen, "so we will swop!"

The Queen and the Cook locked the kitchen door and took off their dresses and hats and crowns and aprons and swapped clothes. (They kept the same petticoats and knickers and boots and stockings.) It was astonishing to see how much the Cook looked like a Queen when she was all dressed up, and it was even more remarkable (and very aggravating to the Queen), to see how much she could look like a Cook.

"No one would know," said the Cook. "I do wish you hadn't got carrot all over the front of this dress!"

"Make the Ladies-in-Waiting give you a clean one," suggested the Queen. "No! You'd better not. That would be very unlike me. You'll just have to put up with it then! What's for dinner?"

"Whatever I get around to cooking," replied the Cook, forgetting for a moment that she was now a Queen. "I've told you and told you I won't have special meals ordered!"

"But I am the Cook now," said the Queen, suddenly realising that at last she could have whatever she chose. "I am the Cook! I can do just as I like!"

"There's more to cooking as them as don't cook imagines," said the Cook darkly.

"There's more to Queening as them as don't queen imagines too," replied the Queen cheerfully. "You'd better go and do what I was going to do next."

"What was that?"

"Sweep out the donkey's stable," said the Queen. "Open the new swimming pool down the road, (I always cut the ribbon and then jump in off the top board so you'd better do the same), come back, put dry clothes on, eat lunch . . ."

"Do you keep the crown on when you jump in?" asked the Cook.

"Oh yes!" replied the Queen. "That's the whole point! That's why I have string on it. To tie it under my chin."

"Oh," said the Cook.

"And don't forget the most important thing."

"What's that?"

"The Royal Donkey of course," said the Queen. "I don't want him bothered."

The Cook sniffed scornfully and said she had no intention of bothering the donkey and the first thing she intended to do as Queen was have a nice sit down. So the Queen went back to her carrot chopping and singing, only this time she sang,

"Lavender's blue diddle diddle
Lavender's green
I'm not actually the Cook diddle diddle but I've
swapped because it's her birthday
I am the Queen."

And after a little while the Cook could endure it no longer. She tied on the crown beneath her chin and went off to look for a stable brush and the next time the Queen looked round from her chopping board she saw that the Cook had gone.

A few minutes later Michael the gardener's boy came tearing into the kitchen.

"The Cook's in the stable," he panted. "She's wearing your crown and sweeping out the donkey's bedroom . . ."

"Did he notice it wasn't me?" asked the Queen anxiously.

"He noticed," said Michael, "and I noticed; but nobody else has said anything at all. The Ladies-in-Waiting are grumbling about carrot stains and the Prime Minister is there with papers to sign and the donkey has gone out into the garden to think and I rushed over in case it was a revolution and you needed help."

"It's only the Cook's birthday," explained the Queen after it had been explained to her what a revolution was and she had thanked Michael for his loyalty and courage. "We've swapped jobs for the day. It's my present to her."

"How kind of you," said Michael impressed.

"Yes, I am a Kind Queen," said the Queen, "but today I am Cook! Lunch and Supper and no snacks in-between, everyone eat what they're given and no grumbling! That's what we have to do for the Cook so that's what everyone can do for me!"

"*Can* you cook?" asked Michael.

"Anyone can cook," said the Queen. "*Cook* can cook after all! I'm going to make chocolate!"

"How?" asked Michael.

"I shall look it up," said the Queen turning the pages of The Royal Recipe Book. "This book is full of chocolate things! Chocolate biscuits, chocolate buns, chocolate cake, rich chocolate cake, chocolate pudding, chocolate chicken . . . chocolate chicken sounds awful!"

"No chocolate, bars of, though?" asked Michael.

"No," admitted the Queen disappointedly.

"Well, I bet we could make it without a recipe," said Michael. "Cocoa, sugar . . ."

"Butter," said the Queen excitedly. "Frozen butter to stiffen it up, cream, nuts for nut chocolate, salt and pepper. Everything has salt and pepper!"

"Delicious!" said the Queen sometime later when all the ingredients had been mixed together in the Cook's biggest bowl. "Delicious!" and she ate another large spoonful. "Or do you think it's too runny?"

"Perhaps," said Michael, and he poured in raisins and dried coconut to thicken it up.

"Cherries?" he enquired, after sampling the new mixture carefully.

"Definitely cherries," agreed the Queen, rummaging in the store cupboard. "Golden syrup?"

"Definitely golden syrup," answered Michael. "Marzipan?"

"Oh, definitely marzipan," said the Queen eagerly.

A long time later a bell rang somewhere in the palace.

Michael and the Queen took no notice.

Then there was a rap at the kitchen door and a Lady-in-Waiting stuck her head round and gasped, "Hurry up with lunch Cook! Queen's getting fractious!"

"Out of my kitchen!" shouted the Queen, just like the Cook.

"Bother!" she said to Michael. "I'd forgotten about lunch! Are you hungry?"

"Not a bit," replied Michael who was full of marzipan and raisins and nuts and cherries.

"Nor am I," said the Queen. "But they will be, especially the Cook. Opening swimming pools is very cold and hungry work!"

The bell rang again. Michael hunted through the cupboards and found bread and butter and a cold cooked rabbit got ready for the kitchen cat. In a moment of inspiration the Queen poured homemade chocolate on the top.

CHOCOLATE CHICKEN wrote Michael on the menu.

BREAD AND BUTTER.

TINNED TOMATOES said the Queen busy with a tin opener.

SURPRISE PUDDING wrote Michael, "That means we can send up anything."

"We'll send up cornflakes and milk," said the Queen. "That will surprise them!"

In the dining room the Cook complained and complained but the Ladies-in-Waiting refused to take any notice. They never complained themselves because, as they truly said, "Anything is better than doing our own cooking."

They ate up the chocolate rabbit and tinned tomatoes and felt only slightly sick. Everyone was very surprised by the pudding, not least the Cook. As soon as lunch was over she marched down to the kitchen.

"Swap back!" she shouted to the Queen who was feeding carrot daisies to the Royal Donkey through the kitchen window.

"I shan't!" said the Queen. "I'm a Kind Queen, but I'm not that kind! You've got chocolate chicken-rabbit all over my front!"

"Well you've got it all over mine!" replied the Cook. "And that there lunch was a disgrace! And the swimming pool was perishing cold and the crown so heavy I nearly sank!"

"Launching ships is much worse than opening swimming pools," remarked the Queen. "Lucky for you it isn't a ship launching day! But there's a garden party at the Treasurer's this afternoon. You'll have to go to that."

"I shouldn't mind a bit of a knees up," said the Cook, cheering up at the thought of a party. "What are you going to do?"

"OUT OF MY WAY AND GIVE ME FIVE MINUTES PEACE!" shouted the Queen, just as the Cook shouted at her every day.

When the Cook had gone the Queen and Michael picked raspberries in the sunshine because raspberry jam was the Queen's favourite and the Cook would never make it.

"And now I know why!" said the Queen after they had picked all afternoon and still not got enough in the basket to make a spoonful of jam. When the bell for teatime rang in the palace they were much too full of raspberries to care about food.

"Anyway it's only the greedy old Ladies-in-Waiting," pointed out the Queen.

"They'll want their tea though," said Michael who had a kind heart and he wrote,

DIGESTIVE BISCUITS

on a menu and sent them up with some teabags.

"They will never know what to do with teabags," said the Queen. "I expect they will eat them."

(But the Ladies-in-Waiting were enchanted with the teabags. They put them under their pillows and kept them for ever.)

"It has been a lovely day," said the Queen late that afternoon. "Cooking is so easy! It's the best job in the world! I wouldn't mind doing it forever!"

"I should hate the washing up," said Michael.

"What washing up?" asked the Queen surprised. "We haven't done any!"

"That's what I mean," said Michael. "There's still supper to get and no clean plates."

"I've got an idea," said the Queen, "and I shan't even think about supper until I've done it because my idea might turn out to be supper. Or it might be a bonfire. I can't tell yet. It's a barbeque!"

"Sausages?" asked Michael, but the Queen explained that what she intended to barbeque was all the rice pudding, all that winter cabbage, all the tinned celery soup, all the liver and kidneys and frozen brussel sprouts that Cook kept skulking in the bottom of the freezer, all the lentils, all the spinach, all the fish paste, and all the cold stewed rhubarb.

The Cook arrived back just as Michael and the Queen were in the middle of their barbequeing, and like many barbeques do, it had turned into a bonfire instead of supper.

"Did you like the garden party?" asked the Queen, cooking away like mad, throwing boiled beetroot onto the bonfire.

"It was awful," complained the Cook, coughing with the smoke. "No crisps, no ice cream, nothing to eat but marmite sandwiches, and then I had to weed the garden afterwards! *Please* swap back!"

"The Treasurer's parties are always like that," the Queen told her. "That's why he's such a good Treasurer; he's so extraordinarily mean!"

"Anyway," said the Cook. 'I've had enough. I don't like it and I want to swap back!"

"CAN'T YOU SEE I'M BUSY!" shouted the Queen as she poked the flames with a broom. "DO I HAVE TO CALL THE LADIES-IN-WAITING?"

That was what the Cook usually said to frighten the Queen and it worked just as well the other way round. The cook retreated hastily back into the palace just as the supper bell rang.

EVEN MORE SURPRISING THAN PUDDING SUPPER, Michael wrote on a menu.

Supper was nothing at all. The Cook complained dreadfully but the Ladies-in-Waiting said at least it was slimming. Michael went out on his bike and fetched fish and chips for himself and the Queen. They ate them beside the bonfire.

"This is the life for me," said the Queen dreamily. "I don't think I shall ever swap back!"

"OH YES YOU WILL!" said a terrible voice.

It was the Cook. She had gone to the box in the attic where she kept her spare things and she had taken off

41

the Queen's dress and crown and put on her spare cook's skirt and hat and apron.

"Now!" she said, marching up to the Queen. "Now there is a Cook and someone pretending to be a Cook and a gap where there should be a Queen!"

The poor Queen went terribly pale at these dreadful words, but better than anyone she knew there could never be gaps. Very slowly she went indoors and took off her apron and put on the crown.

Michael followed after her and tied the string under her chin.

HOME IMPROVEMENTS

One day one of the Ladies-in-Waiting found some money in the street. She dashed into the nearest shop to spend it and came out with a magazine called *Palace Beautiful*. It was full of pictures of the insides of other people's palaces. She took it back home with her and showed it to all the other Ladies-in-Waiting and the Prime Minister and his wife and the Cook and the Treasurer. They looked at the pictures and grew more and more indignant as they realised that never in a thousand years could their palace be called a palace beautiful.

"Something must be done!" said the Prime Minister's wife and everyone agreed. They pounced on the Queen as she happened to be passing through the banqueting hall and announced that they had something important to say to her.

"What sort of something?" asked the Queen suspiciously.

"Nothing but what shouldn't have been said years ago if we wasn't all so soft," replied the Cook, and the

Prime Minister's wife added, "And we're telling you this for *your own good*!" so the Queen knew then that it was going to be nasty.

The Ladies-in-Waiting, who had been getting very impatient, began their complaints at once.

"This palace is too scruffy!" they announced. "It is not posh enough for us at all! None of the rooms look anything like the rooms in our magazine!"

"No they don't," said the Cook.

"Four poster beds and lacy curtains is what we need," said the Ladies-in-Waiting. "En-suite bathrooms so we don't have to queue on the landing, and a proper balcony each and bunches of dried flowers and nice pictures on the walls!"

"We've got nice pictures on the walls," interrupted the Queen looking round at the banqueting hall which was decorated with tapestries and portraits of her dead relations and pictures of donkeys drawn straight onto the plaster and coloured in by the Queen herself.

"Beautiful wishy washy water colours is what we want," said the Ladies-in-Waiting. "And the Cook needs a proper fitted kitchen. Don't you Cook?"

"Fitted into what?" asked the Queen but all the Cook would say was that she had had enough of making do.

"Yes!" said the Prime Minister, "and so have I! How can I be a proper Prime Minister without a great big shining desk and a beautiful huge enormous room full of bookcases and books with gold writing on the covers?"

"But you never read books," said the Queen, surprised, because it was a well known fact that the Prime Minister had been very unclever at school.

"And I need much more room for entertaining," said the Prime Minister's wife.

"What are you going to entertain?" asked the Queen. "Elephants?"

"It is no laughing matter," said the Treasurer and added that he had a few remarks to make about the Treasury and he made them and they were, "The walls are not strong enough, the doors are not wide enough for the money sacks and the windows are too low so that anyone can stare in and see how much I've got."

"Well I think it's a very nice palace," said the Queen.

"So it is," said Michael the gardener's boy.

"So it will be," said the Prime Minister smugly. "I have arranged for the builders and decorators to come tomorrow!"

"And I have arranged a nice Royal Visit to the seaside until it's finished," said his wife.

"And we have packed!" said the Ladies-in-Waiting.

"What about the Royal Donkey?" demanded the Queen, astounded at their cheek. "He would pine if we all went off and left him!"

The Royal Donkey (who had been sneaked in by Michael at the start of the meeting) lowered his eyelashes and nodded sadly in agreement.

"And he hates the seaside," continued the Queen.

(The donkey nodded more pathetically than ever.)

"Kennels?" suggested the Prime Minister's wife. "Most donkeys would be gla . . ."

"KENNELS!" exploded the Queen, while the Royal Donkey suddenly stopped looking pathetic and glared furiously at the Prime Minister's wife, "KENNELS!!! If any one goes into kennels it definitely won't be the Royal Donkey!"

"Oh very well," said the Prime Minister's wife irritably (because the Royal Donkey was smiling at her in a hateful way with half closed eyes). "Oh very well, you think of something! But we can't stay here. It will be uninhabitable!"

"You could camp," said Michael.

"WHAT?!" asked everyone.

"Camp in the palace gardens," said Michael, pretending not to notice the horrified expressions on the faces of the Ladies-in-Waiting and the Prime Minister and his wife and the Cook and the Treasurer. "In tents," he added innocently. "In case it rains!"

"You young hooligan!" said the Cook furiously. "Putting such ideas in her head!"

But it was too late.

"Oh Michael you are clever!" cried the Queen joyfully. "Camping! With tents and sleeping bags and campfire breakfasts and outside baths and all sorts of animals walking in and out all night!"

"Don't even think of it Your Majesty!' said the Prime Minister with desperate earnestness.

"We shall need a huge tent for the Ladies-in-Waiting to share," said the Queen ignoring him. "And another huge one for the Treasurer and his money (you will have to sleep on top of the sacks to make sure no one burgles it), and another small sort of tent for the Prime Minister and his wife, and a little tiny one for the Cook and a beautiful silk pavilion for me and another one for Michael and the Royal Donkey!"

"Oh, I'll stay where I am," said Michael. "I don't need palace improvements!"

"Alright," agreed the Queen. "But you must come and visit us and see the Cook cooking on a campfire and the Prime Minister ministering on I don't know what he will have to use a soap box I suppose, and the poor Treasurer, no locks on tents so he'll be guarding his money all day long, we will have to bring sandwiches to *his* tent . . ."

"Indeed ye will not!" protested the Treasurer. "Sandwiches is no meal for a working man!"

"And goodness knows," said the Queen happily, "how the Ladies-in-Waiting will manage!"

Such a thing had never happened before and people came from all over the country to see the Royal Camp.

The Queen and the Royal Donkey were delighted to show them around, conducting them into the huge messy muddle where the Ladies-in-Waiting slept, pointing out the Treasurer huddled on his sacks and the Prime Minister, horribly exposed to public view, trying to look dignified on a soap box. Everyone's favourite exhibit was the Cook because she made such spectacularly rude remarks when the smoke blew into her eyes. The Ladies-in-Waiting were too dejected to be interesting at all. Nothing seemed to cheer them up except looking at the pictures in their glossy magazine, and they never had very much time for that, the Queen took such a lot of looking after and the Cook made them wash up.

When the Queen and the donkey were not conducting people around the Royal Camp they went and visited the builders and decorators in the palace. The builders and decorators knew a great deal about animals, especially ferrets and pigeons and donkeys. They admired the Royal Donkey very much and told the Queen that all he needed was a pint of stout ever morning to set him up properly.

"Stout?" asked the Queen in surprise.

"Nothing to touch it," the painters and decorators told her and the donkey nodded in solemn agreement. After that he had a pint of stout with his breakfast every morning supplied by the painters and decorators from a big black barrel.

"You must put it on the bill," said the Queen politely, and the painters and decorators said they didn't mind if they did. They were cheerful, friendly people who spent their time drinking tea from mugs and reading newspapers and wondering which horses would win which races, and admiring the pictures on the walls. The Queen did all these things too and enjoyed herself very much.

"Nice little place you got here," said one of the builders to the Queen. "Couldn't be improved on I would say."

"That's just what I think," agreed the Queen, "although I do think a big slide from the turret at the top of the banqueting hall would be exciting and useful: you could watch for visitors from the turret and then scoot down and meet them for tea. The trouble is all the Ladies-in-Waiting hate the idea. And the other thing that needs doing is my bedroom – decorated with postage stamps (in stripes I thought) but nobody else agrees."

"Very long job that would be," said the builder, "and the slide, that would be a long job too."

"Half a mile I should think," agreed the Queen. "I measured it out with string once but nobody would hold the end so it was very difficult."

And she looked so sad that the builders and decorators put down their mugs of tea, stepped over the sleeping Royal Donkey, and went to look for string.

"Take all summer," they agreed at the end of their measuring, "and would cost a fortune, not to mention the price of postage!"

"What does it matter if it *does* take all summer?" asked the Queen. "Camping is lovely and the donkey is so fond of you! And we've got a fortune: the Treasurer goes to sleep on it every night! And," added the Queen trying to look modest, "I get stamps free because of the picture on them!"

After that the improving work began in earnest. The Ladies-in-Waiting perked up as they watched people going in and out of the palace with ladders and string, but they never went to see how things were getting on in case the builders whistled at them. The Queen explained this to the builders who were hurt and offended and said they only ever whistled at pretty people who smiled, and when the Ladies-in-Waiting were told this news they became quite nasty with the Queen. They threw their magazine into the campfire and said it just wasn't worth it. Camping was their worst favourite thing.

It was the Prime Minister's worst favourite thing too, and he said the people would riot before long, seeing their Prime Minister driven to such a state, when in fact the people were quite quiet and nice, not even laughing out loud when they saw his soapbox.

The Treasurer was past complaining, he was so exhausted. The Queen had told the builders that he went to sleep on a fortune every night but that was not quite true. What the Treasurer did was lie awake on it and wait for burglars and it made him very tired.

When it began to rain it was the Cook's turn to have the worst time and she had it very strongly because cooking in the rain for a Prime Minister and a Treasurer and dozens of bad tempered Ladies-in-Waiting was more unpleasant than it is possible to imagine.

When it began to rain the Prime Minister's wife came to the Queen and said she didn't care tuppence for palace improvements and even less for camping.

Meanwhile the donkey and the Queen were having a lovely time. The donkey quickly learnt to turn on the tap of the black barrel of stout with his teeth and was beginning to take an intelligent interest in horse racing, and the Queen was very happy, sleeping in the Royal Donkey's stable when the weather was very bad and sharing the builders' and decorators' sandwiches. It was a sad day for her when they were forced to admit their work was nearly finished, and she did not cheer up until she saw her lovely bedroom and the beautiful slide which ended under a tapestry to give an added touch of surprise.

"That will make the Ladies-in-Waiting laugh," she said, although it sometimes seemed as if they would never laugh again. They told the Queen quite frankly that all they wanted to do was sleep in their own beds in their plain unimproved bedrooms.

"But what about the Cook's fitted kitchen?" asked the Queen.

The Cook stirred her soggy frying pan and said nothing could be less convenient than this dreadful word dreadful word bonfire.

"Yes, well," said the Queen, "but you've forgotten that the Prime Minister's wife wants to entertain elephants and the Prime Minister says he can't be a proper one without a huge enormous posh study!"

"You have entirely misunderstood the situation!" cried the Prime Minister and his wife despairingly.

"But we still need a stronger Treasury," pointed out the Queen. "Ask the Treasurer; he'll tell you."

But the Treasurer shouted from his sacks that by

the time they'd paid the builders and decorators they probably wouldn't need a Treasury at all because there would be no money to put in it.

So the Queen went back to the palace where the builders and decorators had completely finished everything they intended to do. They were taking it in turns to have goes on the slide.

"We hate to go," they told the Queen. "This place feels a proper home-from-home!" and they remarked how much they would like to show it to their wives and children and other relations.

"You have done a wonderful job," said the Queen who had already been down the slide three times on her stomach and was now admiring her stripey bedroom walls. "The palace is beautiful and the donkey is so much fatter and bouncier. You had better give me the bill and I will take it to the Treasurer."

One of the builders took a pencil from behind his ear and a bit of paper from his pocket and he wrote,

ONE HUNDRED AND FORTY SACKS

and gave it to the Queen.

"One hundred and forty sacks!" cried the Treasurer when the Queen gave him the bill and he burst into tears and howled like bagpipes. By the time he had paid it his sacks would be quite flat.

"Less packing!" said the Queen, but he refused to be pleased. Everyone else was very gloomy too, and no sooner did they get back into the palace than they called a meeting in the banqueting hall to complain to the Queen. They pounced on her as she came in from the stables where she had been arranging for the donkey to have his own black barrel installed.

"We have all got terrible colds!" said the Ladies-in-Waiting.

"That's coming into a warm stuffy palace after living in the nice fresh air," remarked Michael.

"We can't see *any* improvements!" said the Cook.

"You would if you looked at the donkey," said the Queen, "and wait till I show you my bedroom and the huge enormous surprise behind the tapestry that I am saving for a huge enormous surprise!"

"And it has used up all the money in the Treasury!" sobbed the Treasurer, blowing his nose on an empty sack.

"Yes BUT I HAVE MADE A PLAN TO GET IT ALL BACK!" announced the Queen. "I AM RENTING OUT THE PALACE TO THE BUILDERS AND DECORATORS NEXT SUMMER! TWENTY SACKS A WEEK FOR SEVEN WEEKS! They are bringing their families and ferrets and pigeons. Of course," she added thoughtfully, "we will all have to move out and I don't quite know where we will go. It *is* difficult with the Royal Donkey!"

There was an awful silence while the Queen tried to think of somewhere they might all go.

"I suppose," said Michael cheerfully, "you could

always camp out in the palace gardens . . ."

The Ladies-in-Waiting and the Prime Minister and his wife and the Cook and the Treasurer all leapt to their feet and rushed at Michael to tell him to be quiet, but it was too late.

"Camp!" cried the Queen joyfully. "With tents and sleeping bags and campfire breakfasts and outside baths and all sorts of animals walking in and out at night . . ."

"They've all fainted!" interrupted Michael.

"So they have," said the Queen, surveying with pleasure the Ladies-in-Waiting, the Prime Minister and his wife, the Cook and the Treasurer, all white as sheets and perfectly silently flat on the floor. "So they have! I wonder why!"

"Excitement!" said Michael.

THE CROWN, THE BURGLAR AND BUDGET

The Queen had a new crown and she hated it. The sharp pointed ends of the diamonds stuck into her head and the spikey gold decorations caught on her hair and pulled.

"It's horrid!" grumbled the Queen.

"Rubbish!" said the Prime Minister's wife who had chosen it. "It's very nice! You ought to be grateful! Plenty of poor people would be very pleased to have a nice new crown!"

"Give it to them then," said the Queen, "and I'll wear my old one."

But the Prime Minister's wife wouldn't and she said the Queen's old crown was a disgrace with its scratches and dents and holes where jewels had fallen out and been lost.

"Not to mention those horrible chewed knobs and the grubby bits of string," she added, jamming the new crown down onto the Queen's head. "At least this one stays on without string!"

"Stays on!" snapped the Queen. "It won't come off!"

That was true. The new crown was so heavy that it sank down over the Queen's head until it came to her ears. When it got to her ears the Prime Minister's wife and the Ladies-in-Waiting folded them flat against her head and pushed the crown down on top. There was a natural springiness to the Queen's ears that stopped it sinking any lower, and there it stuck, very uncomfortable indeed especially as she could not get it off by herself. It took several people pulling on the rim while the Queen cried, "Ow! My Head!" to remove it.

Naturally the people of the country were interested in the new crown, especially as the Queen constantly drew attention to it by tugging at the spikes and asking members of the public if her ears had gone black. She tried to get rid of it on all possible (and impossible) occasions, even, one hot and desperate day, falling accidentally on purpose overboard from the Royal Yacht in the hope that it would come off and be lost for good. So tight and heavy was the crown however, that the Queen stuck upside down in the mud at the bottom of the river and it was such a trouble to fish her out again that perhaps if she had not been wearing such a valuable hat they might not have bothered. Eventually the Queen was retrieved, very muddy and soggy but with the crown still stuck on tight, as bright and sparkly as ever.

The brightness and sparkliness attracted a great deal of attention from the population, especially the more burglarous part. One particular burglar was fascinated by it. Night after night he lay awake in his lair, remembering its beautiful spikey glitteryness and wondering how difficult it would be to burgle the palace. His friends told him that it would be easy and that the palace was filled with people who had more money than sense but the burglar noticed that they did not try and burgle it themselves. His friends said that was only because there was nothing in it that they fancied.

One night the Queen could not sleep. Although they had taken the new crown off, her head still felt sore from wearing it. She bumped around crossly on her pillows and listened to Budget, the Treasurer's dog, howling outside the Treasurer's bedroom door.

"Budget sounds even sadder than me," thought the Queen, and really Budget had every reason to be sad because he lived a very dull life. He spent his time watching the Treasurer count his money and was only taken for a walk once a year. (This was on the day that the population checked the Treasurer's sums, and the Treasurer used to take Budget for a walk in the park to distract them from their calculations. It was a very good plot. It worked so well that the people almost forgot it was *checking the sums day*. They called it Budget day instead, because it was the day they saw Budget, and the Treasurer got away with a lot of wrong answers.)

Anyway, the Queen lay awake with her aching head and thought about poor Budget and wished she could help him, and as she listened she heard the unmistakable sound of a window being pushed up with a screw driver.

"Burglars!" thought the Queen.

Then there came scrabbling noises.

"That's the burglar climbing through the window!" thought the Queen.

Then there was a loud crash and a groan and hopping sounds. "That's the burglar dropping his burglaring tools on his foot!" thought the Queen.

Then there was no sound at all.

"That's the burglar burglaring!" thought the Queen, and climbed out of bed to go and fetch help.

First she went to the Ladies-in-Waiting who were all sitting bolt upright staring into the dark.

"Listen!" whispered the Queen. "Burglars!"

At this word the Ladies-in-Waiting all put their heads under their pillows and fainted on purpose.

"Cowards!" thought the Queen and went to find the Cook, but the Cook was no help at all. She was snoring very loudly and her bedroom smelt deliciously of rum, and when the Queen finally managed to shake her awake all she would say was, "Cor my 'ed!"

"Not much help!" thought the Queen and went off to tell the Prime Minister and his wife about the burglar downstairs.

"Out of my department!" said the Prime Minister and then got down very quickly under the blankets so that none of him showed.

"There's no such thing as burglars!" the Prime Minister's wife told the Queen.

"Didn't you hear the crashes when he climbed through the window?" asked the Queen, but the Prime Minister's wife said all palaces made funny sounds at night.

"Hopping swearing sounds?" demanded the Queen.

"Certainly," said the Prime Minister's wife and ducked down under the blankets beside the Prime Minister.

The Treasurer, who had not yet forgiven the Queen for spending all his money on palace improvements, was very cross when she bounced on his bed.

"Och away to ye bed there's nothing to steal!" he shouted when the Queen asked if he could not hear the silent sound of burglars burglaring and he closed his eyes and went straight back to sleep, snoring like bagpipes.

"It's sometimes very lonely being Queen," thought the Queen, "especially in the middle of the night when there's burglars downstairs."

She went back onto the landing and leaned over the banisters and listened and still she could hear the burglar noiselessly burglaring, and so she fetched the ceremonial and state axe (which was kept in the airing cupboard) (so that it did not go rusty) (because there is nothing worse than being beheaded by a rusty axe) and crept downstairs, and there was the burglar.

"Got you!" shouted the Queen.

The burglar threw his hands up in the air to surrender and then, seeing what the Queen was carrying, lowered them a bit and held his head in place as tightly as he could.

"You're a burglar aren't you?" asked the Queen.

The burglar nodded.

"I knew you were," said the Queen with satisfaction. "I told them so! What are you burglaring?" And she swung her axe around her head a little to remind the burglar to answer quickly and politely.

Realising that he was in a hopeless situation the burglar bowed very low and replied that he had come to burgle her new crown and added (without much hope) that he was very sorry and would never do it again.

"My new crown?" asked the Queen astonished, for she had been very much afraid that he was after her Donkey Diary or her Wellington boots. "My new crown! Whatever do you want that for?"

The burglar replied that it was beautiful and sparkly and was probably worth a mint and that he had looked everywhere and could not find it.

"A plain mint?" asked the Queen cunningly, "or chocolate covered?"

The burglar thought hard for a minute.

"Chocolate covered, a whole box," he replied.

"I'll go and get it," said the Queen eagerly. "It's in a box under my bed! No! You go and get it yourself and then I'll be able to tell them I've been properly burgled and it won't be my fault!"

"Tell who?" asked the burglar.

"The Ladies-in-Waiting and the Cook and the Prime Minister and his wife and the Treasurer," replied the Queen. "They all know you're here! I told them!"

The burglar went even paler then he had when he first saw the axe.

"But they wouldn't believe me," continued the Queen. "The pigs! It would be a good thing if you burgled something from each of them too. They would *have* to believe me then!"

However the burglar, bowing low, said he simply

didn't have time, not if she wanted her crown burgled good and proper in exchange for a box of chocolate mints and the Queen said Oh Alright she would burgle them herself and together they crept up the stairs.

When they reached the landing the Queen pointed out her bedroom and closed her eyes and counted to ten while the burglar went in. Then the Queen tiptoed away and did her own private burglaring and when she finally crept down stairs again there was the burglar parading up and down the banqueting hall in her crown.

"It suits me to a T!" said the burglar admiring himself in a mirror. "I shall never be able to part with it."

"No you won't," said the Queen rubbing her ears feelingly. "Not unless somebody pulls."

"That's a lovely dog you've got there," remarked the burglar, stooping down and patting Budget who had come downstairs with the Queen.

"Yes he is," said the Queen.

"And how did you get on yourself?" asked the burglar politely.

"Brilliant," said the Queen as she unpacked from her dressing gown pockets several pairs of false teeth, a tin opener and a length of string. "I'm glad you like Budget but look what else I've got!"

"A tin opener!" said the burglar.

"Worth its weight in gold, the Cook always says," explained the Queen earnestly.

"False teeth?"

"They belong to the Ladies-in-Waiting," explained the Queen, "and they're always so secretive about them that I'm sure they're very valuable."

"String!" said the burglar.

"It's not ordinary string," said the Queen. "It's the Prime Minister's special string that he practises his tightrope walking on. He tries to keep it hidden. I expect it's worth pounds!"

The burglar looked most unimpressed at the collection of everyone's most valuable possessions but he did not want to disappoint the Queen (and anyway she had forgotten to put down the axe) so he packed them all into his bag, bowed gratefully to the Queen, and began to climb back out of the window.

"Don't forget Budget!" said the Queen. "I'm sure he won't be able to climb out of the window!"

"Budget?" asked the burglar startled.

"This is Budget," said the Queen, pointing to Budget.

"And very nice too," said the burglar.

"You *do* want Budget don't you?" asked the Queen, and Budget laid an imploring paw on the burglar's boot.

"I'm sure I didn't ought to take Budget," said the burglar sounding very shocked.

"You *didn't ought* to have taken anything!" said the Queen sternly, and conveniently forgetting all the things she had taken herself that night. "You *didn't ought* to, but if there is one thing you *should* take it's Budget. He likes long walks and plenty of dinner and you have a kind face and worn out boots so you will do just right!"

And although the burglar protested (feebly, because he really wanted Budget very much) the Queen stroked her axe and refused to listen and in the end the burglar agreed and Budget and the Queen hugged each other goodbye and the Queen let them out by the front door and went happily to bed.

There was great and enormous trouble in the palace in the morning.

"We've been burgled!" cried the Ladies-in-Waiting staring into their empty toothglasses.

"So 'ave I!" groaned the Cook. "Cor my 'ed!"

The Prime Minister discovered his string was gone and cried and cried, and the Prime Minister's wife looked smug and said she was Only Thankful no one was killed, and the Treasurer simply grinned and grinned. Other people's misfortunes always cheered him up and he didn't miss Budget for weeks. The Queen very happily appeared in her comfy old crown at breakfast time.

"Where's your new one?" demanded the Prime Minister's wife.

"Burglared," said the Queen smirking. "I told you there were burglars but you wouldn't listen!"

"This is a terrible day for the nation!" announced the Prime Minister, but it turned out to be not so bad after all. Almost immediately the Ladies-in-Waiting's false teeth were found scattered down the drive and although they had a horrible time sorting out whose were whose they managed in the end. And then the Cook's tin opener turned up, so there was something for lunch after all, and the Prime Minister's bit of string was discovered, tied in a tidy bow to the palace railings.

But the Queen's new crown was never found and neither was Budget. However, a large box of chocolate mints arrived at the palace, addressed to the Queen and with a card that said,

lots of love from B. and B.

and the Queen appeared to think they would do instead. She did not share them with anyone.

OPERATION QUEEN!

There was something wrong at the palace. Everyone seemed to be quarrelling with everyone else. Nobody seemed to be happy and nobody could be bothered. The Ladies-in-Waiting said they had to do *everything* and the Prime Minister's wife said she shouldn't be expected to do *anything*, and the Prime Minister said nothing he did made any difference anyway. The Cook maintained that she wasn't up to getting down to much and the Treasurer simply sulked.

"What is the matter with everyone?" the Queen asked the Ladies-in-Waiting.

The Ladies-in-Waiting did not even bother to reply. They hung around, pretending to be busy but not really working, staring out of the windows and thinking about how bored they felt.

"Everywhere looks so dusty," continued the Queen. "And messy and muddly and dark and disgusting and you Ladies-in-Waiting are so ugly and unsmiley it makes me miserable!"

"Well really!" exclaimed one of the Ladies-in-Waiting.

"Couldn't you tell jokes or sing a bit?" the Queen asked her.

"Sing?" repeated the Ladies-in-Waiting indignantly.

"Yes," said the Queen enthusiastically, "why not? Stand on the table and sing loud funny songs while the others tidy up a bit!"

But the Lady-in-Waiting would not stand on the table and she said she did not know any funny songs and that anyway she had a sore throat.

"Well, stand on the table and smile," said the Queen. "Smile as hard as you can!"

The Lady-in-Waiting replied sulkily that her sore throat was too sore even for smiling and when the Queen (who did not like to abandon her ideas too quickly) ordered her to stand on the table anyway the Lady-in-Waiting said she felt much too weak. And she went to bed and lay there groaning to prove it.

In less time than it is possible to believe all the other Ladies-in-Waiting (who had no intention of standing on the table and singing either), caught sore throats too and by lunchtime they were all in bed, moaning weakly whenever they heard the Queen's footsteps.

"Lazy hussies!" said the Cook coming in with beans on toast at lunchtime. "There's them took to their beds (the idle nothings) and me with my stomach still on my feet!"

"Any pudding?" asked the Queen.

"I don't know how you can mention it," grumbled the Cook, "Not with my stomach like it is!"

"I hate beans on toast," remarked the Queen.

"Leaves me doubled up and screaming as often as not," said the Cook.

"Beans on toast or your stomach?" asked the Queen. "And what about pudding?"

"Pudding?" exclaimed the Cook. "My pudding days are over! It would be Mortal Agony Pudding if I was to attempt it!"

Mortal Agony Pudding was not one that the Queen had ever heard of, in fact it was a very long time since she had had any sort of pudding at all, so she said to the Cook that Any Pudding was better than none and looked around for a spoon.

"There'll be no pudding from me!" said the Cook. "Me nerves are on the verge of collapse! I've been overdoing it and I need complete rest! I shall be Fell Flat Out by teatime unless I get to bed!"

The Queen thought this sounded quite exciting and at teatime she went to see what the Cook looked like when she was Fell Flat Out but there was no Cook in the kitchen and no tea either. There was nothing at all but the sound of faint screams from the Cook's bedroom.

"What *are* you doing?" asked the Queen, having followed the sound of screams to their source.

"Fell Flat Out in Mortal Agony!" the Cook told her smugly. "Just like I warned you!"

"But what about tea?" asked the Queen.

"You'll have to get that good for nothing Prime Minister's wife to do a bit for once," said the Cook.

"I suppose I shall," said the Queen, but when she

went to look she found that the Prime Minister's wife had gone to bed with terrible faint weakness in her legs.

"But I need you to cook,' said the Queen, "and to do all the Ladies-in-Waiting's jobs as well."

The Prime Minister's wife told the Queen it would be the death of her if she did and she showed the Queen her shaking legs to prove how ill she was. Just then the Prime Minister came in and when he was told the situation his legs started shaking too and he climbed into bed beside his wife and said he greatly feared he was past his prime.

"That means there's only the Treasurer left," said the Queen. "I hope *he's* alright!"

But the Treasurer was not alright; he said he had terrible toothache and that anyway he could only cook books, and having explained this to the Queen he wrapped a blanket round his head and climbed into bed and refused to say anything else.

"So now there is only me!" said the Queen. (For Michael was at University learning about donkeys and the Royal Doctor had Gone Private and never been heard of again.) "Only me!" repeated the Queen. "And I shall have to nurse them all better so I had better keep my strength up!" And she returned to the kitchen and got herself an enormous strengthening tea of ice cream and honey and cherries and marzipan and cooking chocolate and pop. After that she went to the stables and fetched the Royal Donkey to live in the palace so that she would have someone nice to talk to, and then she began nursing.

Nursing quickly became the Queen's favourite thing. She had never enjoyed herself so much in her life!

Everyday she packed her patients with hot water bottles to stop them getting chills and then sloshed them with ice cold water to cure their fevers. At night she sang them lullabies to get them to sleep, and no sooner were they asleep than she woke them with trumpet music to make sure they were not dead.

She knotted them into miles of bandages and strapped them down with sticking plaster and every morning she measured them for coffins and wrote all the coffin measurements on neat bits of paper at the end of their beds, like real nurses do.

Down in the kitchen she concocted hot black medicines out of anything she found lying about. Pepper and treacle and mustard were her favourite ingredients but she sometimes added cold gravy to give her patients strength, or curry powder to liven them up. Regularly, three times a day, she went round the beds, pouring her medicines down her patients' throats from the biggest spoon she could find. The Royal Donkey used to follow her, and as he watched them lick the spoon there was an expression on his face that looked to the Queen's patients like a knowing sort of a snigger.

"Do any of you feel better yet?" the Queen used to ask them anxiously, but they alway said no. None of them wanted to be the first to recover. They felt they would rather endure the Queen's nursing forever than get up and do some work, so they lay in their beds and shook their heads and groaned weakly and said what a wonderful nurse they had. All except the Treasurer who said nothing at all.

"Don't you think they should be getting well by now?" the Queen asked the Royal Donkey.

The Donkey nodded violently and trotted off to the library. A few minutes later he came back with a book in his teeth which he spat into the Queen's lap. It was the book about illnesses and the Queen read it all afternoon. That night when she went round with her bucket of medicine she informed her patients that she had discovered what was wrong with them and that she would be curing them in the morning.

"What are you going to do?" they asked in their weak groany voices, but the Queen said she could not tell them in case they worried in the night. She tucked them up very gently and kindly but they couldn't help noticing that the snigger on the Royal Donkey's face was worse than ever.

In the kitchen the Queen assembled the equipment she would need in the morning.

"Pincers for the Treasurer," she told the Royal Donkey. "All he needs is his teeth taking out and he will be good as new!"

The Royal Donkey nodded in agreement.

"The poor Cook has a bad appendix I'm almost sure," continued the Queen. "That should be quite easy! There's a picture I can look at while I chop! Slice her open, snip off her appendix with scissors (wonder what it looks like), sew her up again with string and put a bandage on! I'll practise the sewing on a pillow after tea!"

"About the Prime Minister and his wife," mused the Queen. "Their legs have got too weak to hold them up and you can get awfully good false ones. All I need to do is saw off the rubbishy legs they have now and buy them wooden ones instead! It will be messy," admitted the Queen. "But Worth It In The End!"

The Royal Donkey looked sympathetically excited and the Queen, encouraged, carried on.

"All those Ladies-in-Waiting just need their tonsils taking out! Sharp scissors and a knife, that's all I shall need! I'm going to make a list!"

And she made this list:

TREASURER	TEETH	PINCERS (Practise on cup hooks)
COOK	APPENDIX	SHARP SCISSORS, KNIFE, STRING AND PICTURE IN BOOK (Practise on pillow)
PRIME MIN. AND WIFE	LEGS	SAW (Might be messy) (Practise on chairs)
LADIES-IN-WAITING	TONSILS	SCISSORS AND KNIFE (Nothing to practise on)

That evening the Queen chopped open a pillow and sewed it up again with black string, sawed off some chair legs and pulled several cup hooks out of their sockets. Then she mixed up a bucket of extra strong medicine and went to bed.

Late that night one of the Ladies-in-Waiting (the one who would not sing), came sniffing down to the kitchen looking for something to eat. The first thing she noticed was the chopped up pillow lying on the kitchen table. The second thing she noticed were the sawn off chair legs, and then she saw the cup hooks and the scissors and the sharp knife and the pincers and the saw. And then she found the list.

When she saw the list she shrieked with fright and ran upstairs with it, still shrieking, and showed it to the other Ladies-in-Waiting who (quite naturally) shrieked as well. The Prime Minister and his wife leapt out of bed and came running and so did the Cook and the Treasurer and they read the list and started shrieking too.

There could be no doubt about how the Queen intended to cure them in the morning.

Up in the Royal Bedroom the Queen heard the shrieks and thought drowsily that her patients must be feeling very ill that night.

"But they will soon be better now," she told herself, and stuck her fingers in her ears and went to sleep again.

The Royal Donkey heard the shrieks too, but what he thought he did not say.

Then while the tired Queen slept things began to happen in the palace. In the kitchen the Cook desperately made trifles and puddings and cakes, all beautifully creamed and iced. She made enough for breakfast and lunch and tea and supper and she vowed to herself that she would do the same every night rather than have her appendix removed with scissors by the Queen.

The Prime Minister and his wife, having dusted and polished all the rooms in the palace, helped the Treasurer hang up balloons and streamers that he had bought (with his own money) to decorate the banqueting hall.

The Ladies-in-Waiting were practising comic songs and putting on lipsticks smiles in front of the mirrors. They took it in turns to climb onto the table and dance.

By the time the Queen came down in the morning the palace was transformed. A banquet of a breakfast awaited her on the table, which was polished and sparkling with flowers and silver. The Ladies-in-Waiting were humming and smiling and practising dance steps in corners. They all curtsied most beautifully to the Queen as she came in and the Prime Minister and the Treasurer waved a huge banner that everyone had helped make in the night. It read,

The Cook and the Prime Minister's wife, with their arms around each other's waists, danced a can-can beneath it.

"But you can't be better," protested the Queen. "I haven't finished curing you yet. I was going to operate this morning!"

Hastily the Prime Minister stepped forward and read a long and grateful speech, thanking the Queen for nursing them back to health, and it was so long and so extremely grateful that the Queen stopped feeling disappointed and began to admire her breakfast instead. She couldn't help asking however, if they would not like operating on anyway, in case they got ill again.

"Prevention is better than cure!" she advised with her mouth full of trifle.

But they all said they would not dream of troubling her and when she told them it was no trouble at all, a pleasure in fact, they said they would not dream of it anyway.

After that there were no dusty dismal rooms in the palace, no more beans on toast and no-pudding lunches and no more unsmiling Ladies-in-Waiting. At the first sign of any of these symptoms the Queen would begin enquiring about people's health and the Royal Donkey would look sniggeringly at the patients and they would recover as fast as magic. Even so the Queen never stopped hoping that one day she would be forced to operate. It is hard to say what the Royal Donkey hoped.

THE ACCIDENTAL HAUNTING AND THE BEST ROYAL DONKEY IN THE WORLD

It was nearly Christmas. The weather was freezing. Icy winds blew around the palace all day and all night and the Queen (with much dropping of stitches and knotting of knots and jabbing of needles), had knitted for the Royal Donkey a long stripy scarf with tassels on the end. And the Royal Donkey (who was very intelligent) had learnt to put it on and take it off with his teeth. It was a beautiful scarf and he was very proud of it and wore it nearly all the time and even the Ladies-in-Waiting admired it and wished they could knit.

At that time of the year the Ladies-in-Waiting were much nicer than their usual selves because Christmas was coming and they knew what happened to people who quarrelled. And in the evenings nobody sulked in their rooms or shouted down corridors or pushed rude notes under other people's doors. Instead they gathered together by the fire in the Banqueting Hall and listened to ghost stories told by the Treasurer and the Cook, and in between ghost stories they cheered themselves up by talking about Christmas. It was then that the Queen heard for the first time that Christmas presents were brought by Father Christmas in a sleigh hung with silver bells and drawn by reindeer. This surprised her very much indeed because she had always assumed that Christmas presents were supplied by people's fathers and mothers (or Prime Ministers and Treasurers if they happened to be royalty). But every one assured her that this was just a story made up for children who might be frightened by the thought of Father Christmas sneaking down their chimneys in the middle of the night. And the Prime Minister's wife said that once, when she was very young, before she married the Prime Minister, she had heard silver bells ringing on Christmas night.

"Reindeer bells," said the Prime Minister's wife.

The Queen was more astonished than ever and looked across at the Royal Donkey to see if he thought the Prime Minister's wife could possibly be telling the truth. And the Royal Donkey (who had listened very carefully to the conversation) nodded to show that he thought she probably was.

"I should like to hear the reindeer bells," said the Queen enviously. "When, exactly, is Christmas?"

Everyone looked expectantly at the Ladies-in-Waiting (because what could they possibly be waiting for, except for Christmas?) and the Ladies-in-Waiting looked very silly and sheepish and said that they did not know.

Then there was very nearly a quarrel, and there would have been a quarrel if it hadn't been so close to Christmas. So nobody actually said in plain words how stupid they thought the Ladies-in-Waiting were, and the Ladies-in-Waiting promised to find out and let every one know in good time to hang their stockings up. "You'd better!" remarked the Cook, and the Queen whispered privately to the Royal Donkey that perhaps they should both hang up their stockings every night from now on so as to be sure of not missing Father Christmas, and the Royal Donkey nodded in agreement, and then they sat quietly because the ghost stories were beginning again.

The ghost stories told by the Treasurer were fairly frightful, but they all took place among the wild moors and craggy glens of a distant country, and so were more or less bearable. The Cook's ghost stories were simply appalling and all took place in palaces. What was worse, they had all happened to people who were very well known to the Cook. On the night when it was revealed that nobody in the palace knew the exact date of Christmas the Cook told an especially alarming story concerning the haunting of Ladies-in-Waiting. When the end of the story came the Ladies-in-Waiting were very shivery and quivery indeed and the Queen said she wasn't going to bed that night unless the Royal Donkey could sleep in the room with her. The Ladies-in-Waiting did not like this at all because the Royal Donkey was very untidy in his habits and it was always them who had to clear up the mess afterwards. And, because they were so unnerved by the Cook's story and annoyed by the prospect of the Royal Donkey sleeping in the Queen's bedroom, they forgot it was nearly Christmas and added that the Royal Donkey was nothing but a nuisance and would never dare say boo to a ghost. Everyone went to bed feeling rather cross and jumpy except the Queen (who felt perfectly safe with the Royal Donkey sleeping in her bedroom), and the Royal Donkey (who didn't care tuppence for either ghosts or Ladies-in-Waiting).

Before they settled down for the night the Queen and the Royal Donkey hung up their stockings, huge baggy red ones that had once belonged to the Cook.

"There!" said the Queen when she had finished tying them to her bedposts. "Because it might be Christmas tonight and it would be terrible if we missed it!"

Then she kissed the Royal Donkey goodnight and climbed into bed and the Royal Donkey wrapped his scarf round his neck, curled up on a sheepskin rug and several eiderdowns and mattresses in front of the door, and closed his eyes.

That was the first night the palace was haunted. It was a Lady-in-Waiting who heard the ghost. She said it was the sort of ghost that tiptoes along corridors on high tapping heels and then (after a long time of freezing fearfulness endured by the Lady-in-Waiting), tiptoes back again, sighing softly.

When she first told this story the Treasurer said scornfully that it was nothing to some ghosts he'd heard tell of, and the Cook said it served the Lady-in-Waiting right and had she found out the date of Christmas yet, and the Queen said as casually as she could, "Oh I expect it was just the Royal Ghost," because she didn't want to sound alarmed.

The rest of the Ladies-in-Waiting (the so far unhaunted ones) said it wasn't fair and fancy having to sleep in a palace where that sort of thing went on and they would never feel safe in their beds again and look at the terrible mess that donkey has made and none of them would close their eyes for a wink that night. The donkey did not say anything but he looked at the haunted Lady-in-Waiting as if she was mad.

"And has anyone found out the date of Christmas yet?" asked the Cook that evening in the Banqueting Hall and the Ladies-in-Waiting said how could she be so heartless and that was the least of their worries. So the Cook told them a simply revolting story about a Lady-in-Waiting she had once known who had been such an idle gallivanting good-for-nothing she had been executed for her uselessness.

"And now she gallivants the corridors at night," said the Cook with relish, "tap, tap, tapping in her high heels and sigh, sigh, sighing for her head!"

"How could she sigh without a head?" asked the Queen practically and the Cook (who being a Cook had a good knowledge of anatomy) said you didn't need a head to sigh, it could be done perfectly well with lungs and a windpipe and that was how she managed.

"I'm jolly glad I'm not a Lady-in-Waiting," the Queen remarked to the Royal Donkey as they hung up their stockings that night, and the Royal Donkey agreed.

In the darkness of their dormitory the Ladies-in-Waiting lay awake considering the awful story related to them by the Cook and listening for the ghost in the corridor. And when the palace was perfectly quiet there it came, tapping past their bedroom door. This time the Prime Minister and his wife and the Treasurer heard it as well and they all lay awake trembling until hours and hours of darkness had passed and the ghost returned, sighing a little as it came. And then everything was silent again, except for the sound of pounding hearts, and the peaceful snoring of the Queen.

The next evening (when it became apparent that nobody had yet got around to finding out the exact date of Christmas) the Cook began a story about a wild, lost (dead, of course) Lady-in-Waiting who fumbled barefoot down the corridors rap, rap, rapping with a little hooked stick in search of her missing wits, and everybody told her to shut up.

"I don't know what all the fuss is about," grumbled the Cook, "I'd have thought you'd got more to worry about than ghosts that are nothing more than nightmares come from too much stuffing yourselves at supper time!"

"Stuffing!" exclaimed the Ladies-in-Waiting indignantly because their appetites had completely failed them at the arrival of the ghost. "Stuffing! Wait till it haunts you!"

The Cook did not have long to wait. That very night she was haunted herself.

When the Cook heard the Royal Ghost people became really alarmed because it meant that their last faint hope that it might be a *fake* Royal Ghost was gone. They already knew it couldn't be one of themselves because as soon as the Prime Minister and his wife and the Treasurer had heard the ghost story they had taken camp beds and sleeping bags into the Ladies-in-Waiting's dormitory, so as to all be haunted together. And it was not the Queen playing tricks because all through the frightful nights of haunting they had heard her snoring soundly, so who else might it be? Not the Royal Donkey, who was guarding the Queen and who (whatever his bedroom habits) was undoubtedly loyal. There was no one else.

The Royal Donkey, who in the beginning had been as astonished as anyone by the sudden arrival of a Royal Ghost, was behaving very strangely. Sometimes when the Ladies-in-Waiting were telling their ghost stories he had to rush into dark corners where he shook and hid his face and wiped his eyes on his scarf.

"Fright!" said the Cook, but the Queen, looking closely at the Royal Donkey, saw that she was wrong. The donkey was shaking with laughter, not fright.

"I wish you could talk," she said one night at bedtime as she and the donkey hung their stockings together. "I wish you could talk because I think you know a secret!"

The donkey's shining eyes told the Queen as plainly as words how much he wished he could talk too, but if he knew a secret he kept it to himself.

Then one morning the Cook announced at breakfast, "Tomorrow is Christmas Day and it's a good thing someone's got a brain round here."

"However did you find out?" asked the Ladies-in-Waiting, momentarily distracted from the subject of ghosts.

"I rung the butcher," said the Cook. "And you're a lot of idle hussies not to have thought of it yourselves. That there turkey might have been quacking round the barnyard till kingdom come for all the help I get from you!"

Everyone cheered up very much at the thought of the next day being Christmas until the Treasurer squashed them all at bedtime.

"There's nae use getting excited about whether it's Christmas day tha' morn or no," he remarked dourly. "Him in red'll no come with us awake a-staring and a-staring and a-listening and a-listening and that ye well know. Yon ghost had put an end to Christmas for us and I'll not be hanging up me sporran this year!"

"What?" asked the Queen.

"Father Christmas only comes when people are asleep," translated the Prime Minister's wife, "and how can we sleep in a haunted palace?"

"I sleep," said the Queen, "and so does the donkey so that's all right."

The Ladies-in-Waiting had been saying for days that all they wanted for Christmas was never to be haunted again, but when it came to Christmas Eve and whether or not to bother hanging up stockings they found that this was not true. They wanted presents as well, and they were prepared to sleep through ghosts to get them.

"How do you sleep so easily?" they asked the Queen as she was getting ready for bed, and the Queen replied that she counted donkeys.

"Or Queens or crowns," she added, admiring her reflection in the mirror. "But mostly donkeys."

And she climbed into bed, smiled affectionately at the Royal Donkey, murmured, "One Donkey," and fell asleep.

The Ladies-in-Waiting tiptoed back to their dormitory, clambered over the mess of sleeping bags and camp beds and empty bottles, climbed into their beds, closed their eyes and said hopefully, "One Donkey."

Then they sat up and looked at each other to see if it had worked but it hadn't.

"One donkey is not enough," they said, and they climbed out of bed again, crowded round the mirror to look for inspiration, and decided to count sheep.

"One sheep," they chanted, gazing at the flat shapes of their empty stockings sagging in the shadows, "Two sheep. Three sheep. Four sheep . . ."

Next door the Queen slept soundly, dreaming of sleigh bells.

"Eight hundred and six sheep," sighed the Ladies-in-Waiting (and also the Prime Minister and his wife and the Treasurer and the Cook), "eight hundred and seven sheep, eight hundred . . ."

"It's tonight," thought the Royal Donkey. "Tonight. At last."

"Eleventy hundred and ten sheep," groaned the Ladies-in-Waiting in their sleep. "Eleventy hundred and . . ."

Even the Treasurer had lost count now.

"One sheep," he muttered in his dreams, beginning again. "One sheep-in-waiting. Two ladies in distress. Three pigs in clover . . ."

Nobody noticed when the little Royal Donkey, wrapped in his scarf, pattered down the corridor as he had pattered so many nights before. Down the corridor and out to the Royal Stables he went, because at last it was Christmas Eve. Nobody heard the silver bells blowing in the wind. Nobody ever knew what Father Christmas and the donkey said to each other.

But everyone heard what happened next. The noise that followed woke them all. Pattering and clattering and wild excited braying. It was the Royal Donkey galloping triumphantly back to the palace and noisily celebrating the success of his Christmas secret plan, but it did not sound like that to the haunted ears of the population inside the palace.

"It's the Royal Ghost," whispered the Prime Minister.

"Pursuing the Royal Donkey," added the Treasurer, pale as a haggis.

"What next?" quavered the Prime Minister's wife.

"Us," said the Ladies-in-Waiting, and everyone waited in terror.

"That there donkey is enjoying itself!" said the Cook suddenly, and all at once people realised this was true. If anyone was chasing anyone then it must be the Royal Donkey pursuing the ghost because the braying outside was definitely victorious.

"The brave wee beastie!" said the Treasurer, wiping a tear from his eye, "It's seeing it off the premises!" and the Prime Minister said he'd never have thought it and the Ladies-in-Waiting agreed. And then for the first time everyone noticed that their stockings were a little less saggy and very slightly knobbly and they jumped out of bed in happiness and excitement because it was Christmas morning at last.

The donkey bumped open the Royal bedroom door, paused for a moment at the foot of the bed, and then woke the Queen with gentle kicks.

The first thing the Queen noticed was that there was something different about the Royal Donkey, and the second and third things she noticed (a split second later), were the Cook's old stockings, both of them stuffed and bulging and heaped round with parcels, one for her and one for the donkey. It took all morning to unpack them and although the Queen had never had such a lovely time, every now and then she would pause in her unwrapping to gaze at the Royal Donkey and wonder what the difference was.

Of course everyone told her all about the donkey's Royal Ghost chase, and they said he was magnificent and a hero and they were collecting money to buy him a medal as soon as the shops opened again. There were speeches at dinner about it, and the Ladies-in-Waiting explained how sorry they were for saying the Royal Donkey was a nuisance and wouldn't say boo to a ghost. And the donkey forgave them their unkind words and winked at the Queen, so then the Queen knew for certain what she had already strongly suspected, that the ghost and the Royal Donkey were one and the same.

"Shock," said the Cook when the donkey could not stop laughing, and she did not try to make him help with the washing up. Nobody else escaped however, and the Banqueting Hall was soon empty. Then the donkey curled up under the Christmas tree and fell asleep, and the Queen sat in the tinselly shadows and played with a little silver bell she had found in her stocking, and wondered. And she noticed what was different about the Royal Donkey. He was not wearing his scarf.

The little silver bell was the Queen's best Christmas present. It had been the very first parcel in the top of her stocking. At the time the excitement of getting to the very *last* parcel at the bottom of her stocking had been so great that she hadn't noticed its wrapping. But surely, she thought, remembering, it *had* been unusual? Hadn't it been hay? And why wrap a present in hay unless it was wrapped in a stable? And who would wrap presents in a stable if not the Royal

Donkey? And why would the donkey be in a stable when he had a perfectly good pile of eiderdowns to sleep on on the Royal Bedroom floor? But perhaps the Royal Donkey had had private business of his own there. Something had made him tiptoe there, night after chilly night, all the nights until Christmas to be sure of finding: what?

"He was going to find my Christmas present," thought the Queen, gazing at her little silver bell.

"Father Christmas must have left his reindeer in the stable while he visited the palace. And *this* must be a reindeer bell!" After all, who but a reindeer would have such lovely chiming bells? And the Queen wondered how the Royal Donkey had persuaded the reindeer to part with his bell until she remembered again what was different about the donkey that day.

Was there somewhere a reindeer wearing a stripy knitted scarf?

And the Queen understood then that the haunting of the Royal Ghost had been an accidental haunting by her most loyal and faithful donkey on his way to swap his scarf for a silver bell. Because hadn't she said she would like to hear the bells of Father Christmas's reindeer?

"You are the best Royal Donkey in the world," whispered the Queen, very quietly, so as not to wake him up.